531

This book is due for return on or before the last date shown below.

27 NOV 2006
10 JAN 2011
16 Oct 2a5

EVERYDAY SCIENCE

Under Pressure:
Forces

Ann Fullick

www.heinemann.co.uk/library
Visit our website to find out more information about **Heinemann Library** books.

To order:

 Phone 44 (0) 1865 888066

 Send a fax to 44 (0) 1865 314091

 Visit the Heinemann Bookshop at www.heinemann.co.uk/library to browse our catalogue and order online.

First published in Great Britain by
Heinemann Library, Halley Court, Jordan
Hill, Oxford OX2 8EJ, part of Harcourt
Education Ltd. Heinemann is a registered
trademark of Harcourt Education Ltd.

© Harcourt Education Ltd 2004

Editorial: Sarah Eason and Kathy Peltan
Design: Jo Hinton-Malivoire/Ascenders
Picture Research: Ruth Blair and Debra
Weatherley
Production: Edward Moore

Originated by Ambassador Litho Ltd
Printed and bound in Hong Kong and China
by South China Printing Co. Ltd.

The paper used to print this book comes
from sustainable sources.

ISBN 0 431 16745 1
08 07 06 05 04
10 9 8 7 6 5 4 3 2 1

**British Library Cataloguing in Publication
Data**
Fullick, Ann
Under pressure: Forces. – (Everyday Science)
531.6
A full catalogue record for this book is
available from the British Library.

Acknowledgements
The publishers would like to thank the
following for permission to reproduce
photographs: Action Plus pp.5, 24, 46;
ARSTI/NASA p.30; CORBIS p.48;
CORBIS/Franz-Marc Frei p.14; CORBIS/Gabe
Palmer p.22; Getty 37; Harcourt Index pp. 4,
12, 25, 35; NASA pp. 31, 51; NOAA p.43;
OSF/Keren Su p.41; OSF/Reed p.6; Photodisc
pp. 36, 52; photolibrary.com p.45; Science
Photo Library pp.28, 33; SPL/Colin Cuthbert
p.21; SPL/Dr. Jeremy Burgess p.34; SPL/Geoff
Tompkinson p.38; SPL/Hugh Turvey p.40;
SPL/Jan Hinsch p.18; Sieve Tlyor p.11; Stockfile
pp. 16, 47; The Car Photo Library p.9; Trip/D
Sillitoe, Trip/C Wormald p.32; Trip/M Thornton
p.26.

Artwork by Ascenders apart from Andrew
Quelch p.23; Art Construction p.7; Jeremy
Gower p.19; Mark Franklin pp. 27, 36.

Cover photograph of a skateboarder
reproduced by permission of Rex
Features/Neale Haynes.

The publishers would like to thank Robert
Snedden for his assistance in the preparation of
this book.

Every effort has been made to contact
copyright holders of any material reproduced
in this book. Any omissions will be rectified in
subsequent printings if notice is given to the
publishers.

Contents

Words appearing in bold, **like this**, are explained in the Glossary.

Forces with you

You have just settled down for a good read, but here are a few things to try out first. Jump up in the air. Drop your book – carefully! Walk across the room. Open the door. Stand still upon the surface of the Earth without floating away into space. If you have managed to do all of these things you are already expert at using **forces**.

What are forces?

Forces are pushes or pulls that can change the shape of an object or its movement. They are invisible – but we know they are there because of their effects. Although we cannot see forces we *can* measure them. The unit of force is the **newton** (**N**), named after Sir Isaac Newton, a famous English scientist whose work on forces changed the way people thought about the world.

Forces everywhere

Forces – the pushes and pulls that make things happen – are a vital part of everyday life. Without the force of **gravity** we would float away into space and there would be no life on Earth, as its atmosphere would float away too. Our cars depend on forces to get them moving, to slow them down and to change direction. We do not have to travel in a car to need forces – they are important whenever you move, and the human body has some amazing adaptations that allow it to cope with the forces it meets every day.

Reaching high
Forces on a spectacular scale pushed mountains like these thousands of metres into the sky.

Natural forces, artificial power

Forces are responsible for the very shape of the world around us. The planet Earth is round as a result of gravitational forces. The mountains that shape our landscapes came about because of enormous forces within the surface of the Earth pushing together, and many great valleys have been formed over millions of years by the forces **exerted** by water flowing over them.

Forces in the natural world can be enormous, but forces also work on a very small scale. For example, our ability to hear each other speak depends on forces, tiny pushes that move the working parts of our ears, enabling us to pick up and respond to the sounds all around us.

For thousands of years people have recognized the importance of forces. Even if they have not always fully understood them, they have certainly known how to use them. Fantastic monuments like the pyramids in Egypt, the statues on Easter Island and Stonehenge in the UK were built because our ancestors had developed an understanding of how to use forces to make work easier. That process of using forces to make life easier continues today – you can see it in action around you in everything from a tin opener to a scooter, from the family car to a pair of scissors. We have developed enormous machines to produce forces for us, forces that have enabled us to take over almost every corner of the world, and a tiny piece of space as well.

Detecting and measuring forces

Forces are pushes and pulls. We can detect them and measure them, but only indirectly. What we sense or measure is the *effect* of a force – the change in movement or shape that it causes – not the force itself. We have natural force detectors in our own bodies, and we have developed a range of instruments for measuring all kinds of forces.

Sensing forces
Animals' whiskers are sensitive to forces.

How sensitive are you?

Your sense of touch is vital for letting you know which bit of you is in contact with someone or something else, whether you are holding something soft or sharp. This sensitivity depends on your skin, a massive organ for sensing forces. It covers about two square metres, and contains millions of nerve endings – over 4,000,000 for responding to a light touch, plus thousands more for heavy pressure!

Which way up are you? What position is your body in now? What sounds can you hear around you? Are you moving or not? You can answer these questions because your body is sensitive to forces in the world around you. What is more, the animals and plants who share our everyday lives also have their own force sensors.

Forces in the ear

Sound is made up of **pressure** waves travelling through the air. We pick up the pressure changes through the delicate mechanism of our ears. The pinna, on the outside, collects the sounds. The ear-drum is pushed in by the pressure of the sound waves. It pushes in turn against the small bones in the middle ear, which then push on another **membrane**. When the pressure in the wave decreases, the ear-drum moves out again. This back and forth motion sets up more pressure waves in the fluid in the inner ear, and these are detected by sensitive cells that send impulses off to the brain.

Hearing is not the only force detection that goes on in the ear. The semicircular canals are sense organs in their own right. They give us information about the position of our head, and so are very important to us in keeping our balance. They work because the **fluid** trapped inside them moves in response to forces as we tilt or move our heads, affecting sensitive hair cells. These send information to our brain, where it is interpreted to give us a sense of our position in space.

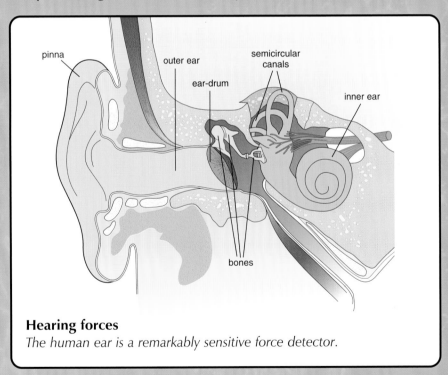

pinna

outer ear

semicircular canals

ear-drum

inner ear

bones

Hearing forces
The human ear is a remarkably sensitive force detector.

Human beings are very sensitive to forces. This makes it much easier for us to cope successfully in our everyday lives. Even in the 21st century, sensitivity to forces is a vitally important part of the human survival kit!

Using instruments

It is great having bodies that are sensitive to different forces, but it is also important to be able to measure forces outside our bodies. Because we cannot measure forces directly, our instruments measure the effect the forces have on things.

The basic instrument for measuring simple forces is the **newtonmeter**. Some newtonmeters are better at measuring pulls, others at measuring pushes. Almost everyone has at least one newtonmeter in their home, although we usually call them weighing scales!

Measuring weight

Everything is made up of a certain amount of material (stuff). This is its **mass**, and it stays the same wherever the object is, even in outer space. But the force anything **exerts** on the surface of the Earth is affected not just by its mass but also by the pull of **gravity** on it (we'll be looking at gravity in more detail later in this book). So if someone lifts you off the ground, they have to overcome the pull of gravity on your mass. This force is called your **weight**. Weight is a widely measured force in everyday life – we watch our weight, we buy food by weight, we prepare recipes by weighing out ingredients, bridges have weight limits. Because weight is a force, it should be measured in **newtons**. Your weight in newtons is approximately equal to your mass in kilograms multiplied by ten.

This is where things get a bit tricky. When we stand on the weighing scales, although they actually measure our weight they are designed to show our mass in kilograms. In science, we have to take great care to use the words mass and weight correctly, which can be difficult because in everyday life we tend to use them incorrectly. For example, in everyday terms we would say a bag of sugar weighs 1 kilogram. However, if we were talking scientifically, and correctly, we would say that the bag of sugar has a mass of 1 kilogram, and its weight on the Earth is 10 newtons. In this book we are looking at the science in everyday situations, so we must take extra care not to get confused.

Measuring forces in a car

As we shall see, forces are responsible for changing movement. Nothing moves at all unless a force acts upon it, and once something is moving it will carry on in a straight line unless another force acts upon it. So when we start our car moving, and drive around in it, we are using several forces.

Use with care
Big forces are involved in moving and stopping a car, and we use very powerful engines and brakes to produce them.

Both speed and direction are important when you are travelling in a car. However, we do not usually measure the exact forces that are being applied at any point as we drive along, we measure the overall effect of those forces. So the speedometer measures your speed, and shows your changes in speed. In other words, when forces make your car accelerate you measure how the speed of the car changes over time.

Detecting destructive forces

Forces make things move and change direction – but they can also be used to make things change shape. Imagine yourself in the kitchen, with a ball of pastry and a rolling pin. By applying force to the rolling pin you can substantially change the shape of the ball of pastry. By squeezing and stretching the pastry you could reform it completely. This is a simple example of the way forces can be used to make things change their shape.

Often these changes are exactly what we want. But if you apply too much force, the pastry turns out too thin, so it tears. Apply too little force and the pastry will be too thick. In the same way, when forces are used in industry, the right amount of force must be used for the desired effect. For example, the metal sheeting used in the bodywork of cars has to be just the right thickness to combine lightness, cheapness and strength. So it is important to have an effective way of measuring the force (pressure) of the rollers that produce the sheets.

Taking the strain!

Sometimes forces acting in one way – making a car move or supporting the weight of a bridge – can have other, unwanted effects. Metals and plastics can be deformed by forces, and these shape changes can be very dangerous. The materials can be weakened and eventually snap, with potentially catastrophic results. So we use instruments to monitor how materials are affected by the forces acting on them, and to give us warning of any problems.

Strain gauges are used to detect potentially dangerous stresses in materials. They are also used to weigh very large objects. A stress is a force that can change the shape of an object, while a strain is the change in shape that happens as a result of the stress. Think of the enormous lorries you see delivering goods all around the country. They travel thousands of miles over roads and bridges, and also across the seas to other countries. For many reasons – safety, cost of ferry crossings, payment for transport – people need to know exactly how much these enormous vehicles weigh. Juggernauts have their own **weighbridges**. The wheels are positioned over strain gauges to work out the force involved and the weight of the whole vehicle.

How do strain gauges work?

In many cases a strain gauge is made up of a wire, or wires, carrying a small electric current. When the strain gauge is affected by a stress – **compressed** or stretched for example – the wire is affected and its **resistance** to the electric current is changed so that more or less electricity flows. This change in the current is picked up by sensors and interpreted in terms of a particular stress.

Some strain gauges are designed to measure compression when an object is squeezed. Others are designed to measure a change in shape when an object is stretched. They can help us measure a wide range of forces and their effects.

Heavyweight vehicles

The forces that the largest vehicles exert on our road surfaces and bridges are immense. Some of the biggest lorries have a **mass** of around 65 tonnes, which is 65,000 kilograms – so their weight is 650,000 newtons. No wonder roads always seem to need maintenance work! Many of them were not built with such loads in mind.

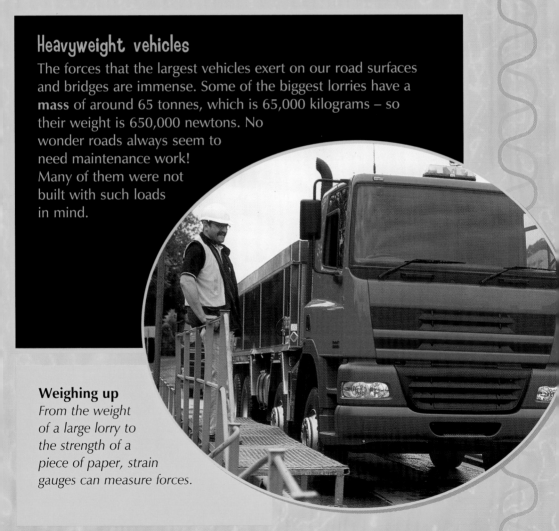

Weighing up
From the weight of a large lorry to the strength of a piece of paper, strain gauges can measure forces.

Measuring natural forces

Walk up to a tree and try to push it over. Then try to lift your family car. Exert as much force as you can – but the tree is probably still standing and the car still firmly on the ground. Generating forces this big is beyond most of us. Yet the wind, the water and the moving continents of the Earth can do these things easily. The forces that can be generated in the natural world around us are almost unimaginably powerful.

Wind power

We have all experienced a windy day, and seen how easily small things are carried away. Many of us have experienced a severe gale, when trees are uprooted and roofs blow off. Hurricanes and tornadoes can flatten whole areas and carry houses, cars and animals far through the air. Wind speed is measured using an **anemometer**, an instrument with cups that are pushed around by the wind. The speed of their rotation is measured and converted into a measurement of the wind speed. The faster the wind, the stronger it is and the greater the forces it can exert.

Tough and flexible
Bridges like this have to have some 'give' to let them safely absorb some of the that high wind.

The Earth moves

The ground beneath your feet and the scenery around you have all been formed by the most powerful forces known to us – the forces generated by the movements of the surface of the Earth itself. The crust of the Earth is a thin, solid layer of rock, floating on a mantle of incredibly hot semi-liquid rock below. This crust is cracked into a number of large pieces called **tectonic plates**, and these are moving about at a rate of a few centimetres each year. If two plates that are sliding past each other get stuck for some reason, huge forces build up until the rocks are suddenly released, moving several metres in a fraction of a second and causing an earthquake.

Measuring earthquakes

Earthquake strength is measured using the Richter scale, which usually ranges from 1 to 9. Each number represents a ten-fold increase in strength. So an earthquake rated as 5 is ten times more powerful than one rated as 4. An earthquake measuring 1 on the scale is detected only by seismographs – we don't feel it. At 7 we have a major earthquake, causing heavy damage and possible loss of life.

Almost everyone is familiar with television images showing the devastation these displays of raw force can bring. In the Los Angeles earthquake in 1994, 57 people died and thousands of buildings were destroyed. The earthquake measured 6.7 on the Richter scale. In areas that are less prepared for an earthquake's devastating effects, the destruction and loss of life are even greater. The earthquake that shook the ancient Iranian city of Bam in 2003 also measured 6.7 on the Richter scale, but it killed an estimated 30,000 people, injured approximately the same number and left around 80,000 people homeless.

The science of prediction

Measuring these immense forces at work is vital for scientists to try to predict when and where earthquakes are likely to happen. They use instruments called **seismographs**. These detect any movement in the Earth and record it. If the Earth is still, the seismograph records a straight line. The greater the forces moving the Earth, the more the trace wiggles about.

Balanced and unbalanced forces

Imagine two teams lined up for a tug of war, with the rope lying on the ground in position. The rope does not move forwards or backwards because nobody is pulling on it. Imagine the teams pick up the rope, take the strain and start to pull – but the marker on the rope remains exactly over the centre point. This time it certainly is not because no one is pulling on the rope – one glance at the straining muscles and red faces of our imaginary teams will show that very strong pulling **forces** are being **exerted** on it. The point is, the pulls in each direction are the same. The forces are balanced, and so no change in movement results.

Now imagine that one team starts to tire. They cannot pull as hard, and slowly the other team heaves the marker towards and finally over their own line. They have won because they were exerting a larger force than the tiring team, the forces became unbalanced and so the rope's movement changed. When forces are unbalanced, things move.

Balanced forces

What happens when forces act depends on their balance. Many things in life stay the same – a book sits on your desk, you sit still on the chair and your clothes stay on the bedroom floor! It is not that there are no forces acting on the objects, but that the forces in different directions are balanced, just as at the start of the tug of war. The **weight** of the book pushing down on your desk is balanced by the force of the desk pushing up on your book (yes, that is really what happens). The weight of you pushing down on the chair is balanced by the chair pushing up on you – the forces are balanced and so nothing moves.

Forces can be balanced even when things are moving – when a car travels along the road at a steady speed the forces that are causing it to speed up are balanced out by the forces that are slowing it down, and so the speed stays the same. When forces are balanced, things stay the same.

Unbalanced forces

Hold out your hand with a book on it – the forces are balanced, with the weight of the book acting downwards and your hand providing an equal and opposite upward force. Now pull your hand away from the book – what happens? The forces are no longer balanced. **Gravity** is still pulling the book downwards but there is no upwards force to oppose it – so the book drops to the floor, where the forces become balanced again.

Unbalanced forces affect the way things move. Unbalanced force starts something moving, and the object will move in the direction of the force applied to it – the book falls straight downwards. If something is already moving when an unbalanced force is applied to it, it may speed up, slow down or change direction, depending on the direction of the unbalanced force.

Pulling together
A tug of war – a great example of the difference between balanced and unbalanced forces.

Speed and acceleration

Riding a bike is a great way of getting from one place to another. What forces are acting on you as you ride along? Anything moving is affected by two opposing sets of **forces** – the forces pushing it forwards and the forces pulling it back. For movement to start the forward forces (**thrust**) must be greater than the forces slowing it down (**drag**).

What a drag

On a bike the thrust is provided by your legs as you pedal forwards. The drag is produced by a very important force – **friction**. Frictional forces are caused by surfaces sticking together as they move past each other. When you are cycling along, the air rushing past you and your bike creates friction. All the time you are **accelerating**, these forces are unbalanced, with your legs producing the larger force – thrust.

Battling forces
Cycling involves a constant battle between the thrust your legs can produce and the forces that drag you backwards.

Fantastic speeds

The fastest people in the world on bikes are all men, because they have a bigger proportion of muscle in their legs than women and so can produce a bigger thrust. Their times are amazing:

- 200 metres   Curtis Hamett   9.865 seconds
- 1000 metres (1 kilometre)   Arnaud Tournant   58.875 seconds
- 4000 metres (4 kilometres) Chris Boardman   4 minutes 11.114 seconds

Once you are cycling along at a steady speed, the thrust and drag forces are balanced. The change comes when you want to slow down and stop. If you are content to take your time over it, stopping pedalling will slow you down because this means that only drag forces are acting, so you will come to a stop. Usually we want to stop more quickly, so we use the brakes. Bike brakes work by increasing the frictional forces acting on the wheels, making it much harder to push them round. By stopping pedalling and squeezing the brakes, you greatly increase the force acting backwards on you and your bike. As a result your bike stops very quickly.

What affects acceleration?

When we are moving, and particularly when we are racing, acceleration is important. So what affects our rate of acceleration? Again it is all down to forces – the size of the thrust, the size of the drag and the **mass** of the object being moved. The acceleration and speed you can go on your bike will be very different to the speed of professional racing cyclists. Speed cyclists try hard to make themselves as **aerodynamic** as possible, so the forward forces are as large, and the backward forces are as small as possible. Professional cyclists also have very strong legs, so they can produce a much bigger thrust. Their clothing, bike and tyres are designed to reduce the frictional forces as much as possible. Finally, the mass of the object being moved is important. Their bikes are built of extremely light, strong materials. You will have seen this effect in reverse if you have ever tried to ride your bike with a passenger, or carrying heavy bags. Extra mass makes it much harder to accelerate, as you need so much more thrust.

Stickability

Imagine going out on a really cold, frosty morning, finding a frozen puddle and sliding on it. Your feet slip easily on the smooth surface – although if you try to walk normally it is not so easy. Now imagine the same place on a dry morning and the situation will be reversed – you can walk OK, but any attempt at sliding is likely to end in disaster. The difference is all to do with **friction**.

Not so smooth
Surfaces that look smooth are actually rough, as this highly magnified picture of a polished metal surface shows.

Slowing down

Frictional **forces** slow down moving objects. The force always acts in the opposite direction to the direction in which the object is moving. They are the result either of solid surfaces rubbing together as movement occurs, or of the **resistance** of water or air to things passing through them. The rougher the solid surfaces are, the more friction there will be when they rub against each other.

As the surfaces rub against each other they generate heat – try rubbing your hands together hard to feel the heating effects of friction. One of the clearest examples of the effect of friction is the difference between cycling on a road, on grass and in sand or mud. The more friction there is between the two surfaces, the stronger the force slowing down the forward movement. Anyone who has tried to cycle along a beach knows that sand is by far the most difficult surface to cycle on.

Overcoming friction

Sometimes frictional forces are a nuisance – they slow things down or stop them when we do not want them to. However, we have developed ways of overcoming friction and keeping things running smoothly. Here is one of them.

Car engines produce the forward **thrust** that allows us to drive around. However, in the engine there are lots of metal parts rubbing together, and although the metal is highly polished and smooth this causes friction. Friction would make the metal parts get hot, expand and stick together. The engine might even explode!

The friction problems in an engine are overcome by using oil. The oil acts as a **lubricant**, keeping the two surfaces slightly apart so they glide smoothly past each other. Oil of varying types and thicknesses is used to lubricate a wide range of machinery. At home we lubricate door locks, sewing machines and bicycle chains, for example. In industry, without lubrication the big machines would grind to a halt.

Lubricating the joints

Swing your arm around from the shoulder – if bone was grating on bone inside your joints, friction would mean the joints would wear out. Fortunately, our joints have two defences:

- The ends of the bones are covered in a smooth, slippery substance called **cartilage** that protects the bone and reduces friction.
- Between the ends of the bones, a liquid called synovial fluid is produced. This lubricates the joint and prevents the bones from rubbing together.

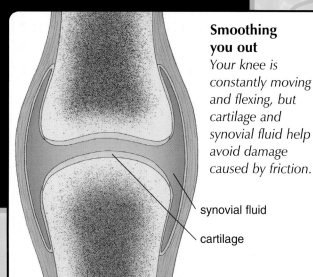

Smoothing you out
Your knee is constantly moving and flexing, but cartilage and synovial fluid help avoid damage caused by friction.

synovial fluid

cartilage

Using friction

There are times when frictional forces are really useful to us.

Friction for stopping

The brakes on your bike use friction to slow you down – the rubber pads press on the rim of the wheel, create friction and slow the wheel. By stopping pedalling, and braking, you stop the forward thrust and increase the amount of friction, so the bike stops quickly. The brakes on motor vehicles work on a similar principle. The frictional force needed to slow a car travelling at 50 mph (miles per hour) is considerable, and the brake pads get very hot when they are applied. Some of their material is worn away every time you brake, so it is important to check them regularly and replace them if they are worn.

Stopping takes time

When a car is travelling at 20 or 30 mph, it takes less braking force to stop it than if it is travelling at 60 or 70 mph. With the same braking force, a vehicle will take longer to stop when travelling fast than when travelling slowly. It will therefore also travel further before it stops. It is vital that drivers leave enough **stopping distance** between their car and the car in front. This distance depends on speed, and so it will change during a journey. Many road accidents are caused by people travelling too close to the car in front. If that vehicle stops suddenly, the car behind cannot stop before the vehicles collide.

Speed	Stopping distance
20 mph	= 12 metres or 3 car lengths
30 mph	= 23 metres or 6 car lengths
40 mph	= 36 metres or 9 car lengths
50 mph	= 53 metres or 13 car lengths
60 mph	= 73 metres or 18 car lengths
70 mph	= 96 metres or 24 car lengths

Using force
If all drivers understood force and remembered to leave these correct stopping distances there would be fewer road accidents.

Making tracks

Tyre treads are vital for maintaining contact with the road, to develop the frictional forces needed for cars to brake effectively.

Talking tyres

Whether on a bike or in a car, your tyres have a major effect on how safe you are. Tyres are the point of contact between your vehicle and the road. The more friction there is between your tyres and the road, the less likely you are to skid.

Safe air

In 1888 John Dunlop, an Irish veterinary surgeon, patented the first inflatable ('pneumatic') rubber tyres.

Inflatable tyres are far safer than the solid rubber tyres that had been used previously because, under **pressure**, much more of the tyre surface makes contact with the road, increasing the stabilizing effect of friction.

On a dry, smooth road surface with no oil on it, the ideal tyres would be relatively wide and completely smooth – just like the 'slicks' used by Formula 1 cars in dry weather. There are several problems with smooth tyres for ordinary cars or bikes. First, completely smooth roads with no oil or grease on them are not very common. Second, in most places it rains sometimes. Water on the road acts as a lubricant and so smooth tyres would slide over the surface, losing almost all of their frictional forces and putting the car or bike into a skid. To make sure they work in both wet and dry conditions, tyres have grooves or **treads** cut into them. These greatly increase the frictional forces if the road surface is wet. The grooves help to push water out of the way of the raised areas of the tyre, keeping it in contact with the road and making braking effective.

Safety in cars

You have probably seen cars presented as exciting, attractive, speedy and desirable. Ask people what they want in a family car and they will probably look for safety, economy – and looks and speed as well. Car designers need a very thorough understanding of the relationships between forces and motion to be able to make cars as fast, attractive, safe and economical as possible.

Good looks and good performance

For a car to go fast, the frictional (**drag**) forces between the car and the air must be as small as possible. Cars with small drag forces are more economical too, because less fuel is needed to produce the thrust required to overcome the drag. So a **streamlined** shape that moves easily though the air is an important design feature.

Coping with collisions

Travelling in cars may well be the most dangerous thing we do. Accidents can happen, sometimes owing to our own carelessness, sometimes because of other drivers. For car designers, this is the vital point – they have to try to ensure that in a collision the people inside the car will be unharmed.

Motorway disaster
In a motorway pile-up like this, good looks in a car count for nothing. It is the safety features that make the difference to the survival of the people involved.

Safety features in cars

crumple zones
In a collision **crumple zones** crumple to absorb the massive energy exerted at impact. They also help prevent damage to the part of the car where you sit.

impact-absorbing bumpers
If you hit something while moving slowly, the bumpers absorb the force of the impact.

airbags
Many cars now have **airbags** that inflate almost instantaneously in a collision. Your body squashes the airbag, which spreads the forces involved over a much wider area and also slows down the rate at which your body stops moving.

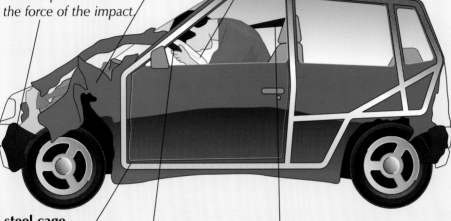

steel cage
It takes an enormous amount of force to deform this rigid steel cage, so it will protect you in a crash.

padding and collapsing steering wheels
In a crash your head or body may hit the inside of the car. Padding and collapsible steering wheels help absorb some forces, so that your body is affected as little as possible.

seat belts
If your car stops suddenly, you will keep moving forwards until you hit something, probably something hard, such as the dashboard or the windscreen. This will slow you down very quickly. Your body will experience an enormous force that might injure or even kill you. Seat belts help to stop this from happening. They stretch slightly as they stop you, so your body is subjected to a much smaller force – and you are much less likely to be seriously injured.

Moving in water

When you walk down the street, there are forces acting on you all the time. One of those forces is the frictional force of **air resistance**. You have to use energy to move your body through the air, although you do not usually notice it. If you are running, or it's a windy day, you might notice the air resistance. But it is a very different story when you try to move in water.

Water resistance

Imagine paddling in the edge of the sea – the water forms splashes and ripples as you move your feet along. Then imagine moving further out – up to your waist – and walking along again. It would soon become tiring, because water is much thicker than air, and so the frictional forces on your body are much greater. The drag would be so great that your legs would begin to ache and you would soon want to get out of the sea. **Water resistance** makes running in the water even more difficult.

Seriously streamlined
Competitive swimmers wear smooth caps and wear full body suits of special material to reduce drag.

Overcoming water resistance

Moving forward, as we have seen, is the result of unbalanced forces where the forward force is bigger than the frictional forces. Because of water resistance, it is hard for a person to move through water in the same way as they move on land. To move easily through water, we have developed different methods of moving. The most obvious way is swimming. When you swim, you make your body shape streamlined. This reduces water resistance as much as possible, so you can move more easily.

Shark shape
The ultimate swimming machine – the streamlined body shape of sharks has changed little over millions of years.

We are not the only animals to move easily through water. Most of us have seen fish swimming around in a tank, a pond, a stream or an aquarium. Fish are beautifully streamlined and can move through the water with ease, usually far faster than any human swimmer.

Building boats

Just as car designers have to understand forces before they can develop safe, fast cars, so boat designers have to understand the forces that act on boats. One important factor is water resistance, so for a boat to move through the water as quickly as possible the hull must be very streamlined.

Fishy birds

Penguins are comically awkward-looking to the human eye. Their bodies are compact, their legs are very short. They are poorly adapted for moving fast over land. As for flying – forget it! Their wings look more like fins, and cannot lift them into the air. But in the water, they are graceful, fast and beautiful. That is what they are designed for – to swim effectively.

Remember what it feels like to play on a see-saw, going up and down, bouncing people up into the air. Remember too how frustrating it was if the two people on the see-saw both weighed the same, and there was no grown-up around to get you started.

Getting moving

The see-saw reminds us of the difference between balanced and unbalanced **forces**. When forces are balanced, nothing happens. If the two children are of equal **mass**, sitting the same distance from the middle of the see-saw, the see-saw will be balanced and will not move unless another force is applied – for example, a downward push on one end by an adult. Once the movement is started, the children can supply a push (force) with their feet when they touch the ground, and keep the see-saw moving.

Balancing act
See-saws are only fun if you get the forces right.

Using levers

If two people who weigh about the same are using a see-saw, they both sit at the ends. However, you can still use a see-saw even if one person is much heavier than the other – an adult and a child, for example. The overall downward force is a result of both the mass of the person and the distance they are sitting from the moving point – the **fulcrum** or **pivot** – of the see-saw. So if the child sits at the end of the see-saw, and the adult sits further in towards the fulcrum, the downward forces will balance out and they can use the see-saw easily. This is the principle of a **lever**.

A lever is a very useful way of lifting something heavy. The heavy object is attached to one end of the lever, close to the fulcrum. A force is then applied to the other end of the lever a long way from the pivot. Even a relatively small force applied to a long lever can lift a very heavy object indeed.

There are many different types of lever, depending on how the fulcrum, the load and the effort are arranged – but they all help us to lift heavy masses more easily and smoothly than we could without them. The wheelbarrow you use in the garden is one example of a lever – the fulcrum is in the middle of the wheel, the load is quite close to the fulcrum and your hands are as far away as possible. The huge cranes used in the building trade are also examples of levers used to lift extremely heavy loads. There is another lever that you use every day – your elbow joint! The load is on your hand, the fulcrum is at the elbow itself and the lifting force is supplied by the muscles that attach the bones of your forearm to your upper arm.

Why levers?

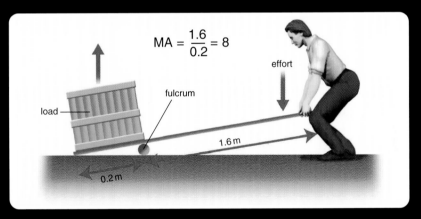

$$MA = \frac{1.6}{0.2} = 8$$

effort

fulcrum

load

1.6 m

0.2 m

Let's calculate the mechanical advantage (MA) levers provide.

$$\text{mechanical advantage} = \frac{\text{length of lever's effort arm}}{\text{length of lever's load arm}}$$

- effort arm = distance from fulcrum to lifting force
- load arm = distance from load to fulcrum

So using a crowbar, you can in theory lift something eight times heavier than you could alone. In practice you will have to 'waste' some effort overcoming **friction**.

Gravity

Everything, if allowed to, falls towards the ground because of one of the best-known **forces** in the Universe – **gravity**.

Essential gravity

Gravity is a force, associated with any body, which pulls everything towards the centre of that body. The most important example in our everyday lives is the gravitational force of the Earth, pulling us all down towards the centre. Without gravity, we would all go floating off the Earth's surface. The atmosphere that provides us with oxygen would float away too. We *need* gravity.

The Earth's gravity was involved in the shaping of the Earth. We only started to understand gravity around 300 years ago. We owe our understanding to a scientist called Isaac Newton and (so the story goes) an apple!

Sir Isaac Newton

Isaac Newton was born on Christmas Day 1642, in Lincolnshire, England. His father had died, and Isaac was born early and was so small and weak that the doctor warned his mother that he would probably die. He survived, and was brought up by his grandmother after his mother remarried. He made a poor start at school – he was more interested in maths, which was not taught, than the Latin and Greek that were. At sixteen he had left formal education and was attempting – very unsuccessfully – to run the family farm. He spent his time reading and working on maths and science problems, while his sheep escaped and damaged his neighbour's crops. Newton even ended up in court!

Isaac Newton
A lonely, rather unpleasant man with few friends, Newton was undoubtedly one of the greatest scientific geniuses ever.

Newton on his genius

This is how, in his memoirs, Newton spoke about his life's work:

 I seem to have been only a boy playing on the sea-shore, and diverting myself in now and then finding a smoother pebble or a prettier shell than ordinary, whilst the great ocean of truth lay all undiscovered before me. 99

Eventually Newton's uncle and old schoolteacher persuaded his mother to let him go to Cambridge University, where he thrived. In 1665 the University was closed down temporarily to prevent the spread of plague, and Newton continued his studies at home. During this time he invented mathematical calculus, did the experiments in which he showed that white light is made up of many colours, and made his famous discoveries about gravity.

The apple story

The story says that Newton was sitting in the orchard when an apple fell on his head. He wondered why the apple fell down rather than up, or sideways – and came up with his theory of gravity. All the evidence we have suggests this story is at least based in fact. Newton often went out into the orchard to ponder tricky problems, and at this point he was trying to determine why the Moon goes around the Earth. An apple falling – although probably *not* on to his head – gave him the idea of a force pulling downwards. He linked that thought to games children played, whirling objects such as balls around their heads on a rope – they seemed like models of the Moon circling the Earth. Putting the two ideas together gave Newton a model of the Moon travelling around the Earth, held in place by a downward force (gravity) – the same force that caused the apple to fall in the orchard. Newton's simple idea would underpin physical science from then, right through to the 21st century.

Gravity everywhere

Although Isaac Newton worked out his laws of gravitation (or 'gravitas' as he called it) in 1665, it was over twenty years before he shared his information with everyone else by publishing it in a book. By then, he had worked out lots of details and some very complex mathematical formulae about it – all of which are still used today.

Everything has gravity

One of Newton's ideas was that everything has its own gravity. It is a strange thought that every object **exerts** a gravitational pull on every other object, but it has been shown to be true. The size of the gravitational force is directly proportional to the **mass** of the object. The only reason that you do not have pencils, rubbers, bits of food and other people constantly attracted to you is because you simply are not big enough. Your gravitational pull is very, very small. It is only when an object is as big and massive as a moon, planet or star that we notice the effects of its gravity.

Different sizes, different gravity

Now we know that the gravitational pull of an object is linked to its mass, we can understand why the gravity on the Moon is so much less than the gravity here on Earth (only about a sixth as strong). It is because the Moon is much smaller and less massive than the Earth. This smaller gravitational force is the reason why we would weigh less on the Moon than we do here on Earth, and why the astronauts who visited the Moon in the 1960s and 1970s could move about so easily, even in their massive spacesuits.

Walking on the Moon
Very few people have travelled in space, but most of us have seen pictures of the American astronauts walking on the surface of the Moon.

Did you know?

A black hole is actually a body in outer space whose mass is so great that the pull of its gravity will not let even light escape.

Earth and Moon

Our Earth exerts a gravitational force on the Moon – and the Moon exerts one back on the Earth. It is the Earth's gravity that keeps the Moon in orbit around us – but how does it work? Keeping one object in orbit around another involves unbalanced forces – otherwise the orbiting object would simply travel away in a straight line. When an object is in orbit around the Earth, the force pulling it towards the Earth (gravity) is set against its forward **velocity**, so that the Moon (or other orbiting body) is always falling towards the Earth but never gets there.

To help explain this, imagine whirling a ball around your head on a string. The ball has forward motion, but the string keeps it moving in a circle around you by exerting a force on the ball that acts towards you. Replace you with the Earth, the ball with the Moon – gravity is the equivalent of the string joining you to the ball.

Swinging round
The Moon remains in orbit around the Earth because of the unbalanced gravitational forces that mean it is always pulled towards Earth but never falls.

The turning tides

When the tide is out it is a long walk to the sea, but if the tide comes in sooner than you expect, your towels get soaked. Gravity is at work: the tidal movements of our oceans and seas are largely caused by the gravitational pull of the Moon. As the Moon circles the Earth, its gravity pulls the sea towards it, producing a high tide. Once it has passed, the sea falls back again to give a low tide. This happens twice a day in most places.

St Michael's Mount, Cornwall, UK
At high tide the Mount is cut off from the mainland. At low tide you can walk across to it. This change in water level is caused by the gravitational pull of the Moon.

Sun and tide

The Sun's gravitational pull also has a weak effect on our tides. At new moon and full moon it works with the Moon to give the exceptionally high **spring tides**. At the first and third quarters it works against the Moon to cause **neap tides**, which are relatively low high tides.

Gravity and you

Gravity is important to all living things on the surface of the Earth, because it keeps us in place. But gravity has other, more subtle effects on our bodies. Our muscles constantly work against gravity to keep us upright and stable. The human body is not a simple shape like a ball or a cube, and we change position all the time. Every time we stick a part of our body out of line, the gravitational forces acting on us change. To stop us falling over, our muscles are constantly making tiny adjustments. We only realize how effective they are when we faint and find ourselves slumped on the floor.

These constant movements against gravity are the reason why it is so tiring being a car passenger on a long journey. The movement of the car as it accelerates, decelerates and turns constantly shifts your body and changes the forces acting to pull it

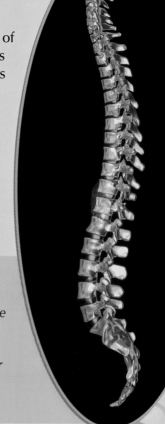

Gravity shields
The cartilage discs between the vertebrae of the spine can be clearly seen as blue discs in this computer illustration.

down. Hundreds of posture muscles have to work to keep you upright, and so you feel tired at the end of the trip. Passengers can feel more tired than the driver, who knows when changes in speed and direction are coming, and who has the steering wheel to provide support.

Incredible shrinking you

Measure your height first thing in the morning and again just before bed. Most people are at their tallest first thing in the morning, and shrink by up to a centimetre during the day. This again is all down to the effect of the Earth's gravity. Between the small bones (**vertebrae**) making up your spine there are pads of rubbery tissue called **cartilage**. Cartilage acts as a shock absorber, cushioning the bones as you move about and jar them, but all day the force of gravity pulls down on your body and the **weight** crushes these cartilage discs. By the end of the day, each one is slightly **compressed** – and the overall shrinkage can be measured. When you lie in bed, gravity is no longer compressing your spine so the cartilage recovers, and in the morning you have gained height again.

Plants and gravity

Think about some plants. They could be trees in a forest, crops in a field, flowering plants in a garden or house plants in a pot. They will all have certain things in common. They will have green leaves and they will be growing the right way up, their leaves up in the light and their roots down in the soil. The colour of the plants is nothing to do with gravity, but the fact that they grow the right way up is another matter entirely.

Dancing plants

Scientists are not sure how plants manage their **geotropisms** (responses to gravity). Some seem to have clusters of starch granules, **statoliths**, in some of their cells. These statoliths are heavy, and fall to the bottom of root and shoot cells in response to gravity. They then appear to affect the way the cells grow, so the plant part grows either towards or away from the direction of gravity.

Growing up

When a seed starts to grow below the surface of the soil it is in the dark. But there is only a limited food store in the seed, so it is vitally important that the new shoot grows up into the light so that the leaves can open and make food. At the same time, the new roots must grow downwards to anchor the tiny plant and take up water and minerals from the soil. Plants manage this because they are sensitive to the force of gravity – the roots grow in the same direction as the pull of gravity and the shoots grow in the opposite direction to it.

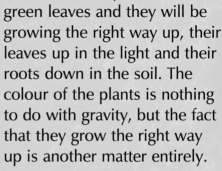

This way up
A miracle of nature – seedlings always come out of the soil the right way up.

Perfect poise
Keeping the centre of gravity in the right place is very important – it can be embarrassing and painful if we lose our balance!

The centre of gravity

The Earth's gravity affects everything on the planet, living and non-living. What is more, everything has one particular point where the effect of gravity seems to be focused, and this is known as the centre of gravity. The centre of gravity of the Earth itself is a point at the very centre of it. Knowing the centre of gravity is important when it comes to balancing. Remember the towers of bricks you used to build when you were small? They start off neat and stable, but as uncoordinated hands add brick after brick they become unstable and fall down.

The same is true of the balances you will have done in gymnastics. You can arrange your body in a variety of positions, and as long as you keep your centre of gravity relatively low and over the bits of you that are in contact with the ground, you are OK. But once the centre of gravity falls outside your anchor points, you lose your balance and fall. The centre of gravity is not just important in gymnastics. Watch a child learning to walk to see how much it matters every time we move.

Overcoming gravity

We are firmly linked to the Earth. The force of gravity makes sure that however high we jump, we always come down again. The same is true for most other living things, but there are some creatures that seem to be able to defy gravity.

Flying force

Airborne
Air has further to travel over the top surface of a bird's wing than the lower surface, so it must travel faster.

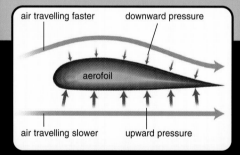

air travelling faster   downward pressure

aerofoil

air travelling slower   upward pressure

A physical law, Bernoulli's Principle, says that fast-moving **fluids** (air is a fluid) have lower **pressure** than slow-moving ones. Therefore the air on top of the wing pushes down on the wing with a smaller force than the air underneath the wing exerts upwards. So there is an overall upward force acting on the wing.

Birds in flight

Watch birds as they fly – they swoop, glide and dart in the air. How do they do it – can they switch off gravity? No, gravity acts on everything. Flying animals simply take advantage of other forces to overcome gravity.

Birds have **sophisticated** bodies that enable them to fly. All flying animals have to be as light as possible. Birds have hollow bones, to give them the lowest possible mass, and enormous muscles to power their wings. They are **streamlined** to reduce the frictional force of **air resistance**. But what really makes the difference is the shape of a bird's wings. They have a large surface area, and the shape of the cross-section of the wings is called an **aerofoil**. This enables the wings to produce a lot of upward force called **lift**, which acts against the **weight** of the bird. It is this lift that keeps the bird in the air and allows it to fly.

Up, up and away

In the natural world there is a limit
to the size of animals that can fly.
Human beings have managed to
overcome those limits and design
aeroplanes that can carry hundreds of
people thousands of metres up in the
air. Even if you have never flown in a
plane, you will have seen them flying
across the sky. Have you ever wondered
how so many tonnes of metal manage to stay
up in the air?

The design of aeroplanes relies heavily on the same
physics that makes bird flight possible. Just like birds, planes are
streamlined to move through the air easily, and are kept as light as
possible with the use of
light, strong metals and
careful design. Also like
birds, planes have wings
with a huge surface area and
an aerofoil cross-section.
The engines have to be huge
to accelerate the plane to a
high speed, in order to get
the air moving across the
wings fast enough to
develop the lifting force
needed for take-off. A fully
loaded airliner, like a Boeing
747-400, with a full
complement of 400
passengers, weighs
3,969,000 newtons, so it
needs a huge amount of lift
to get it off the ground!

Who's who of flight

People have always wanted to fly, but
it took a long time to find out how.

• Ancient Greece: Daedalus and
  Icarus supposedly made wings
  of wax and feathers. Icarus flew
  too near the Sun, the wax melted
  and Icarus fell to his death in
  the ocean.

• **1783** Joseph and Jacques
  Montgolfier flew the first
  hot-air balloon.

• **1903** Orville and Wilbur Wright
  made the first successful
  aeroplane flight.

• **1927** Charles Lindbergh completed
  the first non-stop flight across the
  Atlantic Ocean.

Pressure

Stand on the floor barefoot and think about how it feels. Now stand on tiptoe – the sensations will be very different. This is because by standing on your toes you have increased the **pressure** on the part of your foot left in contact with the floor. Pressure is a squashing or **compressing force**. It depends on both the force that is pressing and the area it is pressing on. To work out the pressure being **exerted** in a particular situation, we need to know the size of the force and the area it is pressing on.

$$\text{Pressure} = \frac{\text{Force}}{\text{Area}}$$

Pressure is measured in **pascals (Pa)** or **newtons/metre^2 (1Pa = 1N/m^2)**

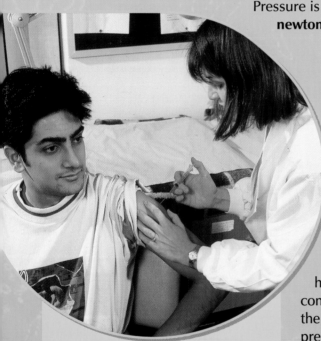

Sharper the better
You want a very sharp needle for an inoculation, because then the doctor has to apply only a tiny force to produce enough pressure to break your skin, and it is almost painless.

High pressure

Imagine trying to hammer a nail into a piece of wood. Everyone knows that you hit the wide end of the nail so that the pointed end goes into the wood, and that the other way round it would not work. Why not? The answer is down to pressure. With the nail the right way up, the force behind your hammer blows is all concentrated on the tiny area of the nail point. This means intense pressure is exerted on the wood and the nail goes into it. If the wide end of the nail is next to the wood, the force of the hammer blow is spread over a much bigger area, the pressure is much lower and the nail will not go in. Having an injection is another situation in which this principle applies.

Monster tyres

The huge tyres of an industrial vehicle spread its enormous weight over the biggest possible area, so it does not get stuck in the mud.

Low pressure

Sometimes we want to reduce the pressure we are applying as much as possible. If you walk in a muddy field you sink in, because the **weight** of your body is acting over the relatively small area of your feet. The farmers who produce our food have to drive massive vehicles in muddy fields to cultivate their crops. If these sink into the mud they can get stuck. Farmers overcome these problems by fitting enormously wide tyres on to their vehicles. These reduce the pressure exerted on the mud and stop them getting stuck. Monster trucks use the same tactics, so do many off-road vehicles and even BMX bikes.

Saving lives

Sometimes understanding how pressure works can save lives. Every year during the winter people fall through the ice on frozen ponds and rivers, and often other people fall through the ice and die trying to rescue them. A little understanding of physics can save lives. The emergency services know that if you stand upright on the ice your weight is pressing down on a small area, which is likely to break. Emergency rescue teams will reduce the pressure – and so the chance of the ice breaking – by lying flat on the ice. Once their weight is spread over a bigger area they have a better chance of rescuing someone safely.

Watch your feet!

One quarter of all the bones in your body are found in your feet. There are around 26 bones in each foot, held together by a network of muscles, tendons and ligaments. Together, all these tissues work to provide you with balance, support and mobility. Your feet are subjected to an enormous amount of force – as you run and jump each foot may have to cope with a force of 2.5 times your body weight.

Feet and forces

For sport, you usually wear trainers or football boots that are specially designed to support your feet. Some shoes, like the 'points' worn by ballet dancers, are designed for very specific activities, while trainers are often worn even when we are not planning a run or a gym session. However, it is easy to forget that many other activities can subject our feet to just as many forces as sport. A day out shopping can involve several miles of walking, while an evening spent dancing involves exercise and foot impact just as vigorous as in any sport. Unfortunately, the shoes we choose to shop or party in are unlikely to be ones that will help to support our feet – we are more concerned about what they look like!

Looking good
People often neglect their foot bones when choosing shoes – yet they have to withstand many forces for hours at a time.

Walking with camels

Walking in soft sand is difficult, because the pressure exerted by our feet means we sink into the sand with every step. Camels manage it very well, however, because their feet are specially adapted – they are very large and spread out widely as the camel treads. This spreads the weight of the camel over a wide area, reducing the pressure on the sand and making sure it does not sink in.

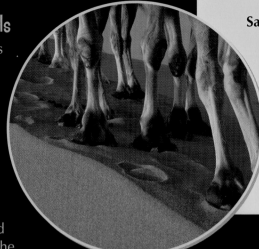

Sandy feet
Camels are much bigger and heavier than we are, yet they walk easily for miles over desert sands.

The right shoes

Why do shoes matter so much? The pressure that your feet experience will vary enormously depending on the sort of shoes you are wearing. You can calculate the difference using your own feet and a couple of pairs of shoes. First calculate the force your body exerts – multiply your **mass** in kilograms by ten to get your weight in **newtons**. Then take several sheets of graph paper. Put your bare foot on one piece and draw around it, to outline the area of your foot in contact with the paper. On another piece draw around a trainer, and on a third piece draw around the areas of a high-heeled shoe that are in contact with the ground. You can work out the area very roughly by counting the squares of graph paper.

Remembering that $\text{pressure} = \dfrac{\text{force}}{\text{area}}$

work out the pressure on your foot if you stand on one leg with bare feet, wearing trainers or wearing high heels. The results can be pretty scary! Trainers spread the weight of your body over a bigger area than even your bare feet, so they reduce the pressure on your foot as you exercise, but the effect of high heels is just the opposite. The bones of your feet are almost always squashed together and cramped, but the pressure exerted when you wear heels to go dancing is potentially damaging, causing problems ranging from blisters to permanent deformity.

Air pressure

We cannot see the air around us, but we certainly use it all the time as we breathe. The Earth's atmosphere extends for miles above our heads, and **gravity** acts on all that air, pulling it downwards towards the Earth. Pressing down on you at sea level is an enormous force of **atmospheric pressure** – 100,000 newtons per square metre, or the equivalent of the weight of a cow pressing down on a dinner plate! The reason we are not crushed beneath the pressure is that the **fluids** inside our bodies exert an equal and opposite force.

Air pressure and human health

Air pressure changes all the time. The amount of air pressing down on us also varies, depending on where we live. People living around sea level experience far greater air pressure than those who live at altitude high up on mountains – almost double in some cases. The 'thinner' air at altitude contains less oxygen than air at sea level, and this can cause real problems for lower-level dwellers who visit or climb mountains.

People who live high in the mountains all of their lives develop bigger lungs with a better blood supply, as well as extra red blood cells, so they have no problems with the low pressure of the air. If you move from sea level to a mountain location you have to give your body time to make more red blood cells to help you extract enough oxygen from the air. The change often results in unpleasant symptoms of altitude sickness which can range from nausea and headaches to a loss of consciousness.

Aeroplanes fly high in the sky and the air pressure up there is very low. This would normally be fatal for us because we would not be able to take in enough oxygen. But the cabins of airliners are pressurized, to keep us comfortable and safe.

Did you know?

When atmospheric pressure increases, gases will dissolve in liquid more readily than they normally do. This is why, when you first open a container holding a fizzy drink, which has been sealed under pressure, there is a rush of gases. They are coming out of solution as the pressure drops.

Finland

Norway

Sweden

United Kingdom

Denmark

Eire

Germany

France

Air pressure and the weather

A **barometer** is an instrument that measures changes in air pressure, either by the movement of a column of mercury or by the changes in shape of a metal box containing air at low pressure. When the pressure is high, it supports a taller column of mercury or squashes the metal box more. Low air pressure supports less mercury or causes less squashing. These changes are transferred to a pointer on a dial showing the air pressure.

Italy

Spain

Many barometers link changes in air pressure to the weather. High air pressure, caused when air sinks and gets warmer as it is compressed, brings fine, cloudless weather. Being warmer, the air can hold more water, so clouds are less likely to form. Just the opposite happens when air at the surface of the Earth rises – the pressure decreases, so the air expands and cools. So low pressure is often associated with cloudy, wet weather.

Air pressure is also responsible for the wandering winds. Imagine blowing up a balloon – creating an area of high pressure – and then letting the air escape. Air rushes out from the high-pressure area into the rest of the room, a low-pressure area, creating a wind. This is how winds blow, from areas of high pressure to areas of low pressure. On weather maps, all areas of equal air pressure are joined together to make lines called **isobars**.

Forces in fluids

Put your finger over the end of a tap or hosepipe while the water is running, and feel the force of the water pushing against your fingers. In the same way, you can feel the pressure of water pushing down on you when you dive down into a swimming pool or the sea. The deeper you go, the greater the weight of water pushing down on you – and water is much denser than air. Once you get down below a couple of metres you will probably start to get uncomfortable sensations in your ears. The increased pressure of the water starts to compress the air in your middle ear and this can feel really painful – you can even end up with a burst ear-drum.

Water pressure under the sea

Because water is so dense, water pressure increases rapidly as you dive. While we can survive thousands of metres above sea level in the reduced air pressure of altitude, we can only go down about 110 metres in water before being crushed to death. What is more, gases get more soluble as the pressure increases. This means that as the water pressure builds up as we go deeper, nitrogen from the air in our lungs can get dissolved in the blood. If we then surface too quickly, this gas can come out of solution again very quickly in the form of bubbles in the blood, which can cause enormous pain and even death. This is called 'the bends'. Think about what happens when you take the top off a bottle of fizzy drink and you can imagine what happens in a diver's blood. The only way people have managed to explore the really deep ocean is by travelling in submarines with specially designed hulls that can withstand the pressure without crumpling. At a depth of around 10,000 metres the pressure of the water is equivalent to having a dinner plate on your head with seven elephants balanced on it!

Safe diving

If you ever go scuba diving, this is how to be sure to avoid 'the bends'. As you return to the surface, keep your eye on the tiniest air bubbles. Make sure you follow these tiny bubbles, or go even slower. That way you will prevent the release of gas bubbles from your blood, and arrive safe at the surface.

Uplifted
Objects float when the upthrust from the fluid is equal to their weight, and that is true for people too!

Archimedes' principle

In the 3rd century BC a Greek king asked the inventor Archimedes to find out if some of the gold in his crown had been replaced with silver, a cheaper but lighter metal. The crown weighed and looked as it should. Thinking about this, Archimedes got into the bath, which overflowed. He ran down the street, shouting 'Eureka!' ('I've got it!'). He had realized he could compare the amount of water displaced by the crown with that displaced by the same weight of gold. If the gold in the crown had silver mixed with it, it would have a larger volume and displace more water. Archimedes tried this out, and sure enough, silver had been mixed with the gold.

Floating and sinking

Imagine yourself floating in a swimming pool, effortlessly drifting with the movements of the water. You are **buoyant**, you float, but how do you stay up? And why, when you are in the water, can you lift people much bigger than yourself – people you would not normally be able to get off the ground? The answer is that the force exerted by the water pushes up on anything lowered into it. This supporting force is known as **upthrust**. Think about getting into the bath – the water level rises when you get in because your body pushes some of the water out of the way – it displaces the water. Upthrust is equal to the weight of fluid an object displaces. Things feel so much lighter or even weightless in water, because much of their weight is supported by the upthrust.

Motion in a curve

Many situations you encounter in physics lessons involve objects moving in straight lines. In real life, things are much more likely to move in curves than to go straight all the time. **Circular motion** has just as much to do with **forces** as any other sort of movement; so what forces are acting to make things move in a curve? As we have already seen, moving objects travel in straight lines if there are no forces acting on them, or if the forces acting are balanced.

Centripetal force

Imagine yourself swinging a ball around your head on a piece of string. The momentum you give the ball in any given direction would keep it travelling in a straight line. The circular movement you see is the result of another force pulling the ball towards the centre. This is **centripetal force**. If the centripetal force disappears – because you let go of the string – the ball will fly off in a straight line.

The level of centripetal force needed to make something move in a circle depends on several things.

Hammer-thrower
Centripetal force acting along its chain keeps this hammer moving in a circle until the athlete lets go.

- The bigger the object's **mass**, the bigger the centripetal force needed for circular motion. This is why small cars corner more easily than large lorries, and why it is easier whirling a ball than a hammer around your head.

- The greater an object's speed, the more centripetal force is needed. A car travelling fast is more likely to leave the road on a corner – it does not have enough centripetal force to keep it going in a curve.

- The smaller the circle's radius (the tighter the curve) the greater the centripetal force needed. Accidents are more likely at tight corners than at wide bends.

Where does centripetal force come from?

When a car is driving around a corner, the centripetal force it needs to keep it on the road is provided by the **friction** between its tyres and the road. The driver uses the steering wheel to change the angle of the front wheels in the direction chosen. The centripetal force develops and turns the car. If not enough centripetal force is developed, the car cannot turn and slides off the road. The situation is made worse when roads are wet or icy – the friction between the tyres and the road is reduced, so that sliding becomes more of a risk.

Cornering on a bike involves just the same sort of forces. Think back to when you were learning to ride a bike. Even when you had mastered cycling in a straight line, cornering still seemed pretty difficult. This is because to get the forces right to enable you to turn the corner, you have to lean into the corner as well as turning the handlebars. If you do not lean enough the bike will not corner – but if you lean too much the bike topples over. Getting the centripetal force just right can be a tricky business!

Easy to miss
Banked tracks help competitive cyclists to develop centripetal forces. Still, they don't always get it right!

Forces and fun

Many of us have experienced the fun (or terror) of some of the massive rides at theme parks – and when we take a heart-stopping 'loop the loop' on a roller-coaster ride we are experiencing circular motion at first hand.

Forces protect you
Thanks to centripetal forces it is actually impossible to fall out at the top of these loops!

Fear, fun and physics

Roller-coasters and other similar rides are set up so that the centripetal forces due to the **acceleration** of the car and the passengers are greater than the acceleration due to **gravity** when the car is at the top of the loop. The result is that we cannot fall out – as long as the ride keeps moving at the correct speed. Theme parks allow us to experience extreme forces, and the ride designers are constantly trying to find new ways to use the forces of circular motion to give us the time of our lives. Even understanding the physics doesn't take away the fear – or the thrills!

Sporting spin

Anyone who is a fan of ball sports will know the importance of spinning a ball. Whether it is rugby or American football, tennis or baseball, snooker or cricket, if a player can get the ball to spin as it travels then the possibilities for success are far greater.

To understand the importance of spin, we need to think about what happens to a ball when it is thrown normally. We launch the ball up into the air so that it travels upwards and forwards. It slows down as it rises, owing to both the pull of gravity and the **drag** effects of the frictional forces of the air. When it gets to the top of its flight, the ball begins to travel forwards and downwards, accelerating because of gravity, but still affected by drag forces.

Spin to win

When someone kicks the ball around the defending wall in soccer, or throws a **curve ball** in baseball, the principle is the same. The player makes the ball spin. Depending on the direction of the spin, the relative air speed is higher on one side of the ball than on the other. This means the **pressure** on one side of the ball, where the air is moving fastest, is less than the pressure on the other side, where the air is moving more slowly – just like the flow of air over the wing of a bird or a plane. So there is an unbalanced force moving the ball in a curve. By varying the direction and speed of the spin they put on the ball, players can vary the amount and direction of the circular motion they set up – and so make it more difficult for opposing players to predict where the ball is going to go.

Artificial satellites

TV and telecommunications satellites depend on circular motion to keep them orbiting the Earth. Once in orbit, they follow a circular path owing to centripetal forces resulting from the pull of gravity. Their speed determines their distance from the Earth; gravity will constantly pull them towards the surface of the Earth, but their curved path will ensure that they stay in orbit.

Forces into the future

Forces play a vital role in our lives, and in future we will find more ways to use them and to overcome their effects.

Safer cars

One of the most risky things most of us do in our everyday lives is to travel in cars. Researchers are pushing forward in all sorts of directions to try to make our motoring safer, and in every case an understanding of forces is behind the developments.

One of the most common injuries in car accidents is **whiplash**. In an impact, particularly if someone runs into the back of a car in which you are travelling, the forces on your body are immense. The seat pushes forward into your back, pushing your spine upright and throwing your head backwards and then forwards very violently. The tissues in the neck and shoulders can be very badly damaged and whilst the injuries are not life threatening they can take a very long time to heal, or leave you with a permanent disability. However, researchers are designing new seats and headrests that mould to your body shape, absorbing many of the forces and holding your head and neck far more successfully.

Safer roads

Many car accidents occur because cars skid. Intensive research is going on into possible new road surfaces to allow greater **friction** between cars and the road. 'Intelligent' tyre designs are also being created to increase friction when braking and cornering, but that reduce friction at high speed.

New parts for old

Lots of research has gone into developing new materials for artificial joints. For example, you have a large range of movement in your hip joint, which also has to bear all the forces as you walk, run and jump. This joint often needs replacing as we get older. The most commonly used artificial hips have a plastic cup fitted into the joint socket in the pelvis, and a metal or ceramic head attached to the top of the **femur** (thigh bone). Unfortunately, most artificial hips wear out in around ten years.

Scientists are working on new materials for longer-lasting joints, such as strong ceramics that can withstand the forces applied to the joint almost as well as bone. Even more excitingly, artificial bone is being developed. This will form a perfect replacement joint, and the original bone will be stimulated to grow around and into it, so eventually it will become part of the body.

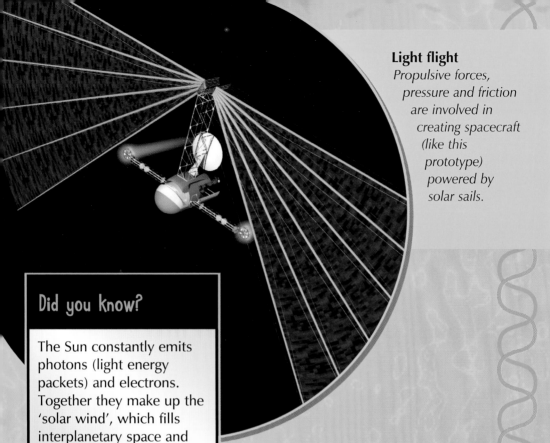

Light flight
Propulsive forces, pressure and friction are involved in creating spacecraft (like this prototype) powered by solar sails.

Sailing into space

Space travel is limited by the time it takes us to travel anywhere and the enormous amount of fuel used. To travel further or faster, new technology is needed to provide the **propulsive** forces. This is where **solar sails** come in.

Scientists are working to produce solar sails that will use the stream of light from the Sun to move spacecraft. A solar sail will be an enormous – around 1 square kilometre – very thin mirror, made of metal-coated plastics or carbon fibres, reflecting the sunlight. The idea is that each **photon** of light hits the mirror, **exerting** a tiny force on it. As there are billions of photons continually striking the sail, the total force will be enough to power a spacecraft. The sunlight will apply a constant **pressure** that will allow the spacecraft to keep **accelerating**, as there is no **drag** in space. So spacecraft will eventually travel at very high speeds without needing bulky fuel. Travelling towards the stars at 90 kilometres per second, a solar-sail-powered explorer could cover the distance from New York to Los Angeles in under a minute, over ten times faster than the Space Shuttle's orbital speed of 8 kilometres per second.

Summary: forces all around us

Forces have shaped our Earth and the Universe. They have dominated life for as long as it has existed on the Earth, yet we have developed a detailed understanding of how they work only in the last few centuries, through the work of scientists such as Isaac Newton. This understanding of the forces in the world around us enables us to use them in a multitude of ingenious ways.

We employ forces in all our methods of transport, on land, water, through the air or into space. We rely on the clever use of forces in sport, from events like the pole vault and the hammer throw, to the football games watched by millions. The gadgets around our home, from the can-opener to the car jack, rely on forces. The industries that make everything we use rely on forces too, for lifting and moving raw materials, parts and finished objects.

Forces are vitally important in nature, for plants and animals alike. Even as you sit and read this book, bone is being dissolved from some places in your body and laid down in others, in response to the forces acting on your skeleton!

Once we know that they are there and what they do, we can find forces at work in every aspect of our lives. The existence and future of the human race depends on them!

Levers and rollers
Today's construction industry uses the same forces that the people who built Stonehenge must have used to manoeuvre these massive stones.

Glossary

acceleration rate of change of speed

aerodynamic designed to reduce wind drag and increase fuel efficiency

aerofoil piece of material on an aircraft etc, shaped to create lift

air resistance force resisting the movement of objects through the air

airbag safety device in cars that inflates on impact

anemometer instrument for measuring wind speed

atmospheric pressure pressure exerted on the surface of the Earth by the gases in the atmosphere

barometer instrument for measuring air pressure

buoyant floats on fluids

cartilage firm, flexible tissue in a human or animal body that maintains shape or protects surfaces from the effects of friction

centripetal force force that pulls (acts) inwards to keep objects moving in a circle

circular motion movement in a circle

compress squeeze (into less space)

crumple zones areas in the structure of a car that are designed to crumple on impact, absorbing much of the energy of a crash

curve ball way of throwing the ball in baseball

drag force resisting the movement of objects through a liquid or a gas

exert bring into use

femur large bone in the thigh

fluid substance that can flow, i.e. a gas, vapour or liquid

force push or pull that causes a change in movement or a change in shape

friction force that affects surfaces in contact with each other, slowing down or preventing movement

fulcrum point about which a lever turns

geotropism movement of plants in response to gravity

gravity attraction between two objects due to their mass

isobar line on a weather map connecting all the points with the same air pressure

lever simple device used to transfer force

lift upward force that acts on objects moving through the air

lubricant substance that reduces friction between two surfaces

mass amount of matter contained in a body

membrane skin-like tissue

neap tides lowest high tides in their fortnightly cycle

newton (N) the unit in which force is measured

newtonmeter instrument for measuring force

newtons/metre^2 (N/m^2) unit of pressure

pascals (Pa) unit of pressure $1\,\text{Pa} = 1\,\text{N/m}^2$

photon packet of electromagnetic radiation energy, such as light

pivot pin on which something turns or swings

pressure amount of force pressing on a given area

propulsive producing forward motion

prototype trial model for use in test runs

resistance force that delays or stops something; not conducting heat or electricity

seismograph instrument for measuring earth tremors

solar sails new method of powering space vehicles under development

sophisticated complex, highly developed for a specific purpose

spring tides tide just after new or full moon when there is the greatest difference betweeen high and low water

statolith solid body in a cell, that seems to respond to gravity

stopping distance distance that a car will travel before stopping after braking at a given speed

strain gauge instrument for measuring the extent to which something changes shape

streamlined shaped to be smooth, offering the least resistance to movement through water or air

tectonic plates large areas of the Earth's crust that move very slowly over the Earth's surface

thrust force acting in the direction of travel

tread patterns in the material of tyres that improve grip on wet roads

upthrust upward force on an object in a fluid

velocity speed

vertebrae small bones making up the spinal column

water resistance force resisting the movement of objects through water

weighbridge drive-on weighing machine for vehicles

weight force with which an object is pulled by gravity

whiplash injury to neck caused by head being jerked violently in a collision.

Finding out more

Books

The Dorling Kindersley Science Encyclopedia, (Dorling Kindersley, 1999)

Groundbreakers: Isaac Newton, by Tony Allen (Heinemann Library, 2001)

Horrible Science: Fatal Forces, by Nick Arnold (Scholastic, 1997)

Science Files: Forces, by Steve Parker (Heinemann Library, 2004)

Science, the Facts: Forces and Motion, by Rebecca Hunter (Franklin Watts, 2003)

Science Topics: Forces and Motion, by Peter Riley, (Heinemann Library, 1999)

Smart Science: Forces, by Robert Snedden (Heinemann Library, 2001)

Websites

www.nasa.gov/topics/shuttle
This part of the NASA website gives some great information about the physics of space travel, which of course involves lots of stuff about forces.

www.euroncap.com
This website is all about car safety and the ways in which safety features are tested.

www.sciencemuseum.org.uk
The London Science Museum website is a great place to find out about all sorts of physics, including forces.

www.crustal.ucsb.edu/ics/understanding
This website gives all sorts of information about earthquakes and how we detect them, as well as listing other sites you might like to visit.

Index

Titles in the *Everyday Science* series include:

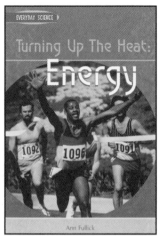

Hardback   0 431 16744 3

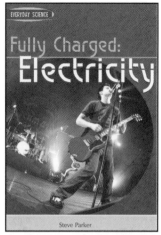

Hardback   0 431 16742 7

Hardback   0 431 16745 1

Hardback   0 431 16743 5

Hardback   0 431 16741 9

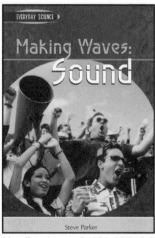

Hardback   0 431 16740 0

Find out about the other titles in this series on our website www.heinemann.co.uk/library